John C. Burrow, William Thomas

Amongst mines and miners

or underground scenes by flash-light - a series of photographs, illustrating

methods of working in Cornish mines

John C. Burrow, William Thomas

Amongst mines and miners
or underground scenes by flash-light - a series of photographs, illustrating methods of working in Cornish mines

ISBN/EAN: 9783742845023

Manufactured in Europe, USA, Canada, Australia, Japa

Cover: Foto ©Suzi / pixelio.de

Manufactured and distributed by brebook publishing software
(www.brebook.com)

John C. Burrow, William Thomas

Amongst mines and miners

'MONGST MINES AND MINERS;

OR

𝕺𝖓𝖉𝖊𝖗𝖌𝖗𝖔𝖚𝖓𝖉 𝖘𝖈𝖊𝖓𝖊𝖘 𝖇𝖞 𝕱𝖑𝖆𝖘𝖍-𝕷𝖎𝖌𝖍𝖙:

A SERIES OF PHOTOGRAPHS, WITH EXPLANATORY LETTERPRESS,

ILLUSTRATING METHODS OF WORKING IN CORNISH MINES.

— ⋅⟨⋅⟩⋅ —

Part I.—An Account of the Photographic Experiences,

BY

J. C. BURROW,

Photographer to H.R.H. the Prince of Wales.

Part II.—A Description of the Subjects Photographed,

BY

WILLIAM THOMAS,

ASSOC. M. INST. C.E., F.G.S.,

*Formerly in the Mining Association and Institute of Cornwall; Lecturer in "Mining" and "Testing of Ores," and
Instructor in "Mine Surveying," at the Camborne School of Mines, &c.*

LONDON:
SIMPKIN, MARSHALL, HAMILTON, KENT & CO., LIMITED,
STATIONERS' HALL COURT, E.C.
CAMBORNE:
CAMBORNE PRINTING AND STATIONERY Co., LD.

1893.

WATERLOW AND SONS LIMITED, PHOTOGRAPHIC ART PRINTERS, LONDON WALL, LONDON.

CONTENTS.

ILLUSTRATIONS.

PREFACE.

DURING a long experience as a photographer in the most active mining district of Cornwall, I have often been intrusted with the preparation of photographs of mines and mining appliances for lantern, or other educational, uses at the Camborne Mining School, for book or catalogue illustrations, and for general purposes. Mr. W. Thomas, the Secretary to the Mining Association and Institute of Cornwall, and one of the leading spirits of the Mining School, first suggested to me the idea of extending my experience in mining photography to underground workings, and I am deeply indebted to him for his valuable assistance in carrying the idea into practice. I am desirous of expressing my thanks also to Capt. Josiah Thomas, of Dolcoath Mine, Capt. Charles Thomas, of Cook's Kitchen Mine, Capt. C. F. Bishop, of East Pool, and Capt. J. Richards, of Blue Hills, and to the agents in these mines, for the facilities they have afforded and the help they have so kindly given. Mr. W. Thomas has further increased my indebtedness to him by volunteering to write a descriptive account to accompany the photographs selected for publication.

The many difficulties experienced in carrying out the work will be a sufficient apology for the incompleteness of the series, or the lack of systematic arrangement in the order of the views. It is a rather disheartening experience to find that the results of a whole day's work with an energetic band of helpers are not "printable," but such experience was mine on more than one occasion. The work, however, is so full of interest, and its performance so productive of welcome enlightenment on many critical points, that I have no intention of allowing it to remain where it is. I hope that at no distant date, the present attempt may be followed by another and more successful one.

J. C. BURROW.

CAMBORNE, *November*, 1893.

'MONGST MINES AND MINERS.

PART I.

HOW THE CAMERA WAS USED.

By J. C. BURROW.

DVANCEMENT in any particular branch of science is often slow and laborious, and, if examined in detail, the progress is not very apparent. When, however, the distant Past is contrasted with the Present, it is evident that great strides have been made and important revolutions effected. This applies as much to the photographic as to any other branch of applied science; for, although the results of daily researches and experiments may not be very striking in themselves, yet, were our fathers in photography, of forty or fifty years ago, to revisit the scenes of their labours, they would be more than astonished at the present high standard of pictorial work. One is apt to be satisfied with the attainment of any special object, regarding it as the *acme* of human effort. But there is no standing still, and what seems perfect to-day will be superseded to-morrow.

To the scientist, the engineer, and the explorer, the camera has become an absolute necessity. It has been used in all kinds of places, on the surface, under the sea, in the air, and even under the earth's surface. The greater the difficulties encountered, the stronger the determination has been to accomplish successful results. Usually the indispensable light comes direct from the Sun, but that is of course unable to penetrate the rocky crust of mother earth. Hence the first difficulty in underground photography is to satisfactorily illuminate the workings by artificial means. The objects of the following sketch are to describe how this illumination may be effected, and to illustrate the advantages which the artist may take of the illumination.

After preliminary trials with cameras varying in size from 10 × 8 to half-plate, it was finally determined to use the latter because of its lightness, portability and moderate size, the latter being specially important in confined situations. The light bellows Kinnear form of camera was most suitable. Double dark slides were used carrying fourteen plates, but such were the difficulties experienced that often five or six plates only could be exposed on the same day. When changing plates underground there was no danger of their being damaged by the light, for when the candles were extinguished there was absolute darkness. But, since it was impossible to keep one's hands clean underground, it was found better to take the plates well protected in dark slides. Lenses of all descriptions were tried, with more or less success. The rapid symmetrical did very well for certain subjects, and a half-plate portrait combination was fairly good when used in an open place where the subject did not require great depth of focus. Care was, of course, taken to prevent the flare spot. The ordinary wide angle was much too slow. A lens having all the advantages of each of these was required, one that would embrace a wide angle, give depth of focus, and speed. This was found in the Zeiss' Anastigmat, Series III., made by Messrs. Ross & Co. It proved to be a perfect gem, and with it splendid results have been obtained, both underground and at surface. A sliding tripod stand was most convenient. Sometimes the camera had to be tilted at an angle of 60°, and the front leg tied to a rock to prevent overbalancing.

At other times it was strapped to a ladder, or a bar, looking down an inclined shaft, or fixed on the ends of a couple of stout planks over a yawning "gunnies." The sliding form of tripod allowed the greatest freedom in such situations.

The best apparatus manufactured is of no practical value without good plates. On this subject, so important to the photographer, pages might be filled with the experiences of a twelvemonth underground. The plates of several makers were tried, slow plates, rapid plates and isochromatic plates. But none equalled the Cadett lightning plate. At first all the candles were extinguished, as the halo round each spoiled the effect of the picture, but, with the lightning plate, every miner was taken in his working position, with his light in its usual place. So sensitive were these plates that the camera had to be well covered to prevent any stray pencil of light being admitted other than through the lens. This requires careful attention when working in daylight. The diaphragm slit in the lens, even, should be covered, say, by means of a wide indiarubber band.

It is needless to detail the incidents attending the transport of apparatus from surface to the bottom of an inclined shaft half-a-mile below. Some were unpleasant, many were amusing. Occasionally the band of willing helpers was recruited from certain classes of individuals totally unaccustomed to mining and mines. Readers intending to attempt underground photography must not be discouraged when a too eager assistant, staggering through the semi-darkness with a hydrogen cylinder of 20 feet capacity under his arm, and a pair of lime-light burners in one hand, stumbles headlong into a pool of water by the side of the level. Nor must they lose their self-control when, after carefully selecting the driest spot available to open the magnesium powder tin for re-charging the lamps, a "flash" of water from some unknown source falls into the tin as soon as the cover is off, instantly "dropping the curtain" most effectually upon the remainder of the day's programme. The temptation to place on record many incidents, annoying at the time of occurrence, but extremely interesting as reminiscences, becomes strong. On one occasion, just as arrangements for a first shot of the camera were completed, a strong voice, some ten fathoms overhead, shouted, "Hallo, down there. "Fire." "*Don't* fire yet," was the reply. "We *have* fired. Go back under the stull." Too late to postpone matters, the only thing left to do was to ask, "How many?" "Three. Look out." In a few moments, bang, bang, bang went three holes, the roar of falling stuff followed, and a few loose stones rattled down the foot-wall to the place where the camera had been fixed. This meant waiting for a long time for the atmosphere to regain a sufficient degree of clearness, and, of course, refixing the whole of the apparatus.

The preparations required were more extensive than one imagines. Each helper undertook a particular duty. One adjusted the lime-light burners, another attended to the oxygen and hydrogen cylinders and trappings, another prepared the magnesium lamps, and so on. The writer, after repeated unsatisfactory experiments with different flash-lamps, designed a pair of triple-flash lamps, which have proved exceedingly useful and have given most satisfactory results. The high temperatures of the deep mines caused camera and lens to be covered with condensed vapour for some time after the scene of operations was reached, a source of much bother.

A state of readiness having been arrived at, the word to "light up" produced a powerful flash from the lamps and ribbons simultaneously. The lime-lights were previously at their maximum intensity. An exposure of from two to four seconds generally gave the best results. If everything appeared favourable in the strong light, another subject was sought; for a second exposure, in the same place, on the same day, rarely

---

* When a hole is charged ready for blasting it is customary for the miners who are responsible to give a warning to all who may be in the immediate vicinity by shouting, "Fire."

gave good results, owing to the "fog" caused by the products of the combustion of the magnesium. For close subjects two triple-flash magnesium lamps were generally used, so placed as to destroy shadow as much as possible, but in large areas, such as that shown in Dolcoath Man Engine Shaft (No. 2), more lamps were brought into requisition. In such places the air was generally cooler and clearer, and sometimes two exposures in succession gave fair results under such circumstances. The bottom of the shaft in Cook's Kitchen Mine (No. 18) was a difficult subject. The temperature there was 100° F. The miners work nearly naked. The camera was attached to the ladder and tilted at an angle of 45°. Water dropped everywhere and came from the foot-wall in a steady stream. Heat, water, and vapour, combined with the peculiar setting of the camera, made the work tedious and difficult.

In the foregoing the writer has attempted to sketch an outline which may guide one desirous of commencing experiments in this new channel for photographic enterprise. Very little has been done in this direction so far. The Freiberg and Clausthal mines have each produced a series of plates of close subjects, and Mr. H. W. Hughes, of Dudley, has obtained some excellent results in the coal and limestone districts of South Staffordshire. Apart from these and the productions of Mr. Arthur Sopwith, also in coal mines, attempts at underground photography have not generally been successful. So many difficulties have presented themselves at the outset that the work has invariably been abandoned after brief trial.

SECTION OF DOLCOATH MAIN LODE.

Scale of Fathoms.

PART II.

A DESCRIPTION OF THE SUBJECTS PHOTOGRAPHED.

By W. THOMAS, Assoc. M. Inst. C. E., F.G.S.

———

OOK illustrations of underground operations and appliances are, like some drawings intended to represent adventures in books of travel, apt to be highly coloured, and a few sensational pictures of miners in impossible, but, to the uninitiated, "fetching." positions have undoubtedly often helped to promote a transaction in which both book and buyer have been "sold." It is not, however, so easy to agreeably misrepresent the real in honest photographs. This fact has long been appreciated, not only by the artist, who finds it essential to elaborately "touch up" his productions in order to meet the harmless desire of the public to have their good looks exaggerated, or at least emphasised, but by the artist's patrons, whose gallant struggles to make

"The worse appear the better"

frequently have tragic ends. The writer's friend, Mr. Burrow, has succeeded in obtaining an excellent series of representative photographs in Cornish mines, at surface and underground, and has been persuaded to re-produce a portion of these in book form. The writer has, with much pleasure, attempted to briefly describe the plates selected for re-production, although it seems unnecessary, in the majority of instances, to explain that which has been rendered sufficiently clear by the quality of the picture, from an artist's point of view, and the judicious selection of the subject, from a mining standpoint.

A brief reference to the frontispiece may well precede a description of the underground photographs. It represents the group of mines on the north side of Carn Brea Hill, as seen when looking east from the top of the north stamps engine-house at Dolcoath. A reduced skeleton of the photograph has been engraved, and numbers inserted to render the most important details more distirct. (*See* page 14).

1. The old stamping engine at Dolcoath. This was erected to deal with the early output of tin at the time when it was becoming evident that the shallow deposits of copper were to be replaced at greater depths by similarly productive deposits of tin. The rapid development of Dolcoath into *the* great tin mine of the world necessitated the erection of two other engines for increasing the stamping power as time passed on. It is from the top of the house which contains one of these engines that the photograph is taken.

2. The new Californian stamps at Dolcoath. In 1892 it was again decided to increase the stamping power, and 40 heads of Californian stamps were added. Additional dressing appliances were constructed to treat the tinstuff from the new stamps. Electric light is employed.

3. An engine here pumps water from a shaft close by for dressing purposes, and has plenty of spare power for stone-breakers which are to be added.

4. Dolcoath Eastern Shaft. (*See* Section.)

5. The Dolcoath valley smithy, where Trevithick is said to have performed much of the work required for the construction of his first locomotive. The original roof was destroyed by fire a few years since, but a new roof was placed on the original walls, and the building is still used as a smith-shop by Dolcoath Mine.

6. Cook's Kitchen Mine office. The oldest "count house" in Cornwall.

7. Cook's Kitchen Mine pumping and winding engines.

8. Cook's Kitchen Mine stamps and dressing floors.

9. New Cook's Kitchen Mine.
10. Tincroft new pumping engine.
11. The north part of Tincroft Mine.
12. Carn Brea Mine, south part.
13. Carn Brea Mine, north part, showing the new pumping engine.
14. East Pool Mine in the distance.
15. Carn Brea Castle.
16. Carn Brea Monument.

The illustrations are taken from four mines, Dolcoath, Cook's Kitchen, East Pool and Blue Hills. A short statement of a few facts concerning each of these mines may be of some interest.

DOLCOATH.*

It is impossible to say how long this remarkable mine has been worked. "A tradition remains that in 1788 the aggregate produce, mostly of copper ores, had already realized *two millions* sterling; but in that year the adventurers—believing they had extracted everything worth removal—abandoned the mine, which had reached a depth of 185 fathoms."†

The present Company was formed in 1799, and, during the first half of the present century, calls amounting in all to £45,252 were made. This sum represents the total amount subscribed by the shareholders since the operations were resumed in 1799. The result is phenomenal. Between that year and 1867 the produce realized £3,087,832, while the profits divided in that period amounted to £309,395. Since 1867 the profits have been very largely increased, and, including the dividend of £1 per share

---

* Dol-côth, the old field or meadow : the old valley or dale. The name of a great mine in Camborne, Cornwall. Pryce's *Mineralogia Cornubiensis*, p. 320. Published in the year 1778. A more probable derivation is *dol* = a pit (modern Welsh *twll*, a hole) and *coth* = old. Dolcoath = the old pit or mine.

† Henwood, in *Transactions of The Royal Geological Society of Cornwall*, Vol. VIII., Pt. I., p. 447.

(there are 4,700 shares) declared on October 30th, 1893, the total dividends since 1799 amount to about £920,000. For many years Dolcoath has been a tin mine, but the early profits were made on copper. At various times in the history of the mine considerable quantities of other metals including silver, nickel and cobalt, have been found.

By the kind permission of the Manager, Capt. Josiah Thomas, the interesting longitudinal section of the main lode which Capt. Thomas issued to the shareholders at the end of last year, is here re-produced. It has been brought up to date for the occasion, and is self-explanatory. The extent of the workings will be understood when it is stated that there have been 75 miles of levels driven in the mine. (*See* page 12).

Previously to 1828 the workings had been so extensive that in that year a subsidence occurred affecting a large area. Henwood* refers to this and describes the movement as slow, and one which occupied several weeks. "After it had ceased, some thousand loads of timber were used for keeping open the requisite communications ; in some cases, however, it was deemed unsafe to attempt propping the overhanging sides of the larger cavities, until inaccessible and dangerous crags had been brought down by cannon shot."

Amongst the several interesting objects which remind one of the venerable antiquity of the mine, the beam of the 85 in. Cornish pumping engine on the Engine Shaft deserves notice. This beam was cast in Waterloo year, 1815, by "William's Perran Foundry Co.," the date appearing with the maker's name, including the "e," in embossed cast-iron letters on the side of the beam. *Lean's Engine Reporter* for March, 1893, records the quantity of water raised by the engine in that month as 185 gallons per minute. Assuming this to represent the average quantity of water raised since the battle of Waterloo was fought, (the engine has

---

* *Transactions of The Royal Geological Society of Cornwall,* Vol. VIII., Pt. 1., p. 666.

worked continuously from that time), the extraordinary total raised in the
period indicated amounts to 33,859,000 tons, a volume sufficient to fill a
cube whose side measures 350 yards. The mine employs about 1,300
hands. The engine shaft is being sunk below the 425 fathom level.

The Manager's statement at a recent meeting of shareholders that
"the lode at the deepest level is the richest we have ever had" naturally
gives great satisfaction to the residents in the parish of Camborne, in
which the mine is situate, and of which, it is needless to add, it is the
mainstay.

COOK'S KITCHEN MINE.

Tradition says that a tinner named Cook once upon a time
discovered a kindly lode and commenced to work thereon with excellent
results. To all friends who inquired how things were going at the mine,
Cook, it is said, invariably replied favourably, and added "the lode is
as wide as my kitchen." Hence the rather curious name, "Cook's
Kitchen," by which the oldest, and second deepest, Cornish mine is
known. No one knows when the mine was first started. It has
certainly been working without a day's suspension for 150 to 200 years.
Unfortunately of late years it has had little to boast of, except its
antiquity, for no dividends have been declared since 1871. As a copper
mine few Cornish mines have been more successful. Some hundreds
of thousands of pounds sterling were given in dividends while copper ore
was produced. The mine is situated immediately to the east of Dolcoath,
and is worked on the same lodes. The section of the main lode in
Dolcoath shows the great ore body in that mine to be dipping eastwards,
and the hope that a continuation of it may ultimately be found in Cook's
Kitchen has encouraged the shareholders to continue operations. The
engine shaft has recently been completed to the 420 fathom level below
adit, the latter being about 28 fathoms under the surface.

During the last century there were three enormous water wheels at work, one being underground. Two of these were maintained in working condition up to a comparatively recent period. Pryce writes in 1778, "The water engine wheel, at Cook's Kitchen Mine, is 48 feet diameter, and works her tiers of pumps of 9 inches bore, which being divided into four lifts, draws eighty fathoms under the adit. If the stream of water were sufficient to fill the buckets of the wheel, she would draw forty fathoms deeper with the same bore." *

EAST POOL.

This mine, situated about midway between Camborne and Redruth, also has a remarkable history, but as operations were commenced only in 1834, the charm of antiquity has not enabled the mine to gain the popularity enjoyed by Dolcoath, its wonderful productiveness notwithstanding. The total amount subscribed by the shareholders has been less than £3,000. The expenditure of this sum has enabled the executive to divide over *half a million* sterling in profits and to purchase and erect the existing extensive machinery for prosecuting the mine. The profits at the present time amount to about £8,000 a year. The association of minerals in East Pool is most interesting. Tin has been, and is, the main product, but copper, arsenic and wolfram are still raised, and, at various times in the history of the mine, cobalt, bismuth, uranium and other metals have been produced in appreciable quantities. The engine shaft is sunk vertically about 300 fathoms from surface, and in addition to the pitwork, it accommodates a double skip-road, probably the most efficient in the county. The miners are raised and lowered in this shaft by a two-deck cage. The number of persons employed is about 730.

* *Mineralogia Cornubiensis*, p. 151.

BLUE HILLS.

This mine is situated in one of the most interesting mining districts in the world, St. Agnes. It is one of the oldest mining localities of Cornwall ; some of its deposits of tin have been remarkable for their richness and extent, and the complicated series of heaves caused by the intersections of veins of several different ages has afforded to many generations a most attractive study. Henwood in his *Observations on Metalliferous Deposits*, gives a quotation from Borlase which at once illustrates old-time mining in St. Agnes, and the productiveness of the deposits worked.*

Blue Hills is separated from Polberro by Penhalls, a portion of which has recently been added to Blue Hills sett. The badly faulted belt of ground traverses these mines. The heaves are, however, more numerous and complicated in Penhalls and Blue Hills than in any of the surrounding mines. These heaves will be referred to later on.

RAISING AND LOWERING MINERS.

For many years the excessive mortality amongst Cornish miners formed a subject for serious consideration and discussion, both in the county and out of it. Several papers dealing with the matter have

---

* The quotation runs :—" The richest tin-mine I have ever heard of, as to the quality of the ore, is one in the parish of St. Agnes . . . . called Polberro. Several parallel and contiguous veins, mostly of large-grain crystals, make the treasure of tin in such quantity, that, in the year 1750, they could not get horses enough to carry the tin from the mine to the melting-house, but carried it in ploughs" (wains drawn by oxen), "a very unusual sight (though doubtless a more effectual and easy draught, where the ways will admit of wheels). Great part of the ore was so rich that it need not to be stamped, and the lode was so large that it afforded vast rocks of tin ; one rock, in March, 1750, was brought to Killinick melting-house near Truro, which weighed 664 lbs., and it brought 11½ for 20, in the stone ; [another] weighed 1200 lbs.'—Borlase, *Natural History*, p. 188.

2.—The Man Engine at Dolcoath Mine.

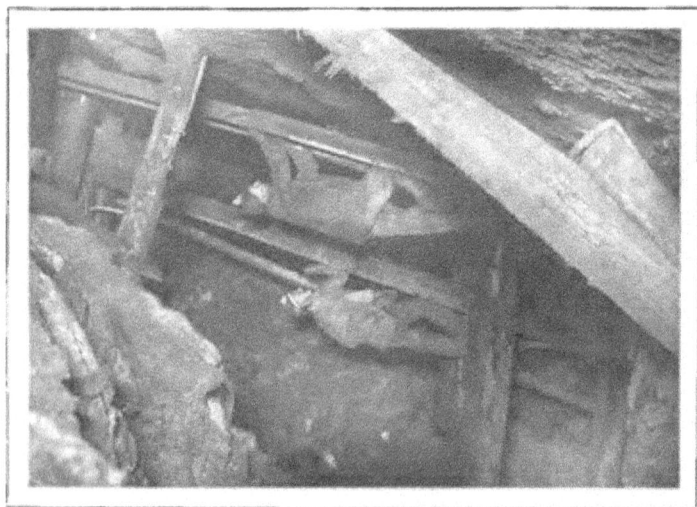

1.—The Man Engine at Cook's Kitchen Mine.

been carefully prepared and one of the most interesting of these was read in 1880 by the late R. S. Hudson, M.D., of Redruth, who devoted much time to the systematic study of the subject.[*] Amongst the several causes which contributed to the high death rate the principal were, undoubtedly, the accumulation of particles of carbon in the lungs, the result of the use of the miners' candle for lighting purposes, and of powder for blasting. But another important cause was the state of exhaustion daily produced by climbing to and from work on the ladders. Although the miners' candle is as popular as ever, powder has given way to nitro-glycerine compounds, and the gig or cage has in many cases replaced the ladders. These changes have, together, produced a more satisfactory condition of affairs. Mr. Thurstan C. Peter, the Superintendent Registrar for a district which covers the large mining parishes of Camborne, Illogan, Redruth, Gwennap, &c., recently stated at a meeting of the members of The Mining Association and Institute of Cornwall,[†] that he had taken some trouble to look back over the death registers for a great many years, and he was perfectly satisfied that the Cornish miner was, every year, living longer than he used to. The registers for the last fifteen or twenty years proved that the increase in the age of miners dying was very extraordinary. This is very gratifying. It can, moreover, be readily understood, for the conditions under which the men work in the mines have been wonderfully improved.

No. 1.—THE MAN ENGINE AT COOK'S KITCHEN MINE.—This was taken 156 fathoms below the adit, or about 215 fathoms below the surface. The Man Engine Shaft has been sunk to the 170 and the man engine has been carried to the 134. In addition to the accommodation provided by the man engine, a gig to carry six men was put in the engine shaft in 1888, and as this takes men direct to the deepest point in the mine,

[*] "Smoke, in Relation to the Health of Cornish Miners," by R. S. Hudson, M.D.— *Proceedings Mining Institute of Cornwall,* Vol. I., p. 288.

[†] March 2, 1893.

it has naturally become more popular than the man engine. The photograph shows one man standing on a step of the engine which is just below one of the sollars* or platforms fixed in the shaft at intervals of 12 feet, and on which the miners stand while the engine makes the return stroke. A second man is on the ladders which are usually fixed by the side of the man engine from top to bottom. In the background is the pipe which conveys compressed air to the deeper workings for use in connection with rock-drills, an air-winch, and for ventilating purposes.

NO. 2.—THE MAN ENGINE AT DOLCOATH MINE.—This was taken at the 234 fathom level below adit in Dolcoath.† It shows more clearly the arrangement of sollars in a man engine shaft. The underlie of the lode, too, is clearly indicated by the inclination of the engine rod. An iron coll fixed behind the rod on the bottom sollar shows a method of supporting and guiding rods in an inclined shaft. The rods are of wood and are joined by strapping plates and bolts. A joint made in this way is illustrated in the photograph, the lower end of the strapping plate appearing underneath the centre sollar.

The man engine usually makes about five strokes per minute, thus enabling the miner to ride 60 feet per minute. This speed may be doubled by using double rods. There are, however, no double rod engines at work in the county at present. The single rod engine remains in use in three or four mines only, and a few years more will see it altogether replaced by gigs or cages.

NO. 3.—THE BALANCE BOX.—Where long lengths of rods are used it is necessary to counter-balance their weight. This is done in Cornwall by the balance box, which is attached, by means of a connecting rod, to the main rod. In an inclined lode the appliance is often constructed so as to lean over until it has attained the underlie of the lode. The only way of obtaining a photograph was to get over one of these, in an open place and fix the camera to look down on the top of it. This will explain the rather curious appearance of the picture. The balance box is fixed at the 236 fathoms level in Dolcoath Man Engine Shaft, and the plane in which it works is the same as that of the lode, the underlie of the latter at this point being about two feet in a fathom.

Within the last five or ten years gigs or cages have been placed in many of the deep mines in Cornwall. The capacity of the gig has been governed by the size of, and accommodation afforded in, the shaft. Most

* Sollar.—Celtic Cornish Soler = a stage of boards in a mine. Sel = a foundation. Cp. Modern Welsh Sail.

† The adit in Dolcoath is nearly 30 fathoms below the surface.

4.—CAGE AT DOLCOATH.

3.—BALANCE BOX AT DOLCOATH MINE.

of the shafts being old and small, the gigs as a rule are consequently of limited capacity. In some mines, however, gigs to carry 10 to 16 men have been constructed; for example those at Botallack, East Pool, Carn Brea, and Wheal Agar.

No. 4.—Gig at Dolcoath.—This photograph shows a portion of the skip road at the 302 in the Eastern Shaft, with a single-deck gig capable of carrying six men. The man engine takes the miners to the 314, but, as will be seen on referring to the section of Dolcoath, the Man Engine Shaft is in the western part of the mine. A small gig in the Eastern Shaft has been found convenient for the men working in the eastern part of the sets.

BREAKING GROUND.

Various terms are applied in different mining localities to the getting, or winning, of the contents of a bed or vein. The Cornish miner talks of breaking ground, or of stoping. The sinking of shafts is followed by the driving of levels and crosscuts, and the sinking and rising of winzes[*] or communications between the various levels. These constitute the exploratory or development section of the work. The exploitation is by means of tutwork or tribute. In the former the miner is paid a given price per fathom, or per ton, for work done. He is paid by measurement or weight. The tributer is paid according to the quality of the veinstuff he breaks, careful assays of his stuff being made in order to determine its value to the mine. Both tutworkmen and tributers work in "pares"[†] or companies of from two to twelve usually. In a few instances a single individual takes a pitch on tribute, and where the hardness of the lode necessitates blasting, he uses a small hammer, of 4 to 5 lbs. weight, when boring a hole. The miners' hammer, however,

---

[*] Winze is old Celtic Cornish for a short underground shaft, perhaps derived from GWYNYS, pierced.

[†] Pair.—Any indeterminate number of miners who work together in a mine in a pitch upon tribute, &c. Pryce, *Mineralogia Cornubiensis*, p. 325. Par, Celtic Cornish for a company.

generally weighs about 7 lbs., and requires both hands to use it
effectually. Where two men work together, one turns the borer and the
other uses the hammer. In the mines working on hard lodes there are
often two hammers to one drill, the "pare" being composed of three
men, as illustrated in plates Nos. 5 and 6.

No. 5.—THE 355 STOPES, COOK'S KITCHEN MINE, LOOKING WEST.—The hanging-
wall of the lode is very plainly indicated. Staging of the usual temporary nature has
been erected to enable the men to approach the roof.

No. 6.—AN "UPPER," EAST POOL MINE.—Holes have to be bored in all
positions and directions. A hole bored vertically upwards is called an "upper," and it
is one of these which is illustrated in the picture. It is not an easy thing to effectually
"beat an upper," and young miners who are adroit at "uppers" naturally are apt to boast
of their dexterous use of the hammer. A hammer or pick standing on end is often
made to do duty as a candlestick.

In connection with an Exhibition of Mining Machinery, organized
by The Mining Association and Institute of Cornwall in 1888, there was
a hand-boring contest at Camborne which attracted considerable attention.*
Only one "pare" of three men from any one mine was allowed to com-
pete. A large block of granite of uniform hardness was obtained and
firmly bedded in a convenient position. Eight minutes were allowed each
"pare"; all were to use steel of one inch diameter, but the size and
shape of the "bits," or cutting edges, were left to the discretion of the
competitors. The prizes were awarded for the following results:—

Prize.	Mine.	Depth bored.	Time.	No. of blows per minute.
1.	Tincroft .	13 inches	6 min. 43 secs.	91
2.	Dolcoath .	12½ ,,	7 ,, 18 ,,	130
3.	Carn Brea	12⅞ ,,	8 ,, 0 ,,	117
4.	South Crofty .	11½ ,,	8 ,, 0 ,,	112
5.	Cook's Kitchen	9½ ,,	8 ,, 0 ,,	107

The Tincroft men were the only ones who "slung round" when striking.

---

* Transactions of The Mining Association and Institute of Cornwall, Vol. II.,
Pt. 2, page 21.

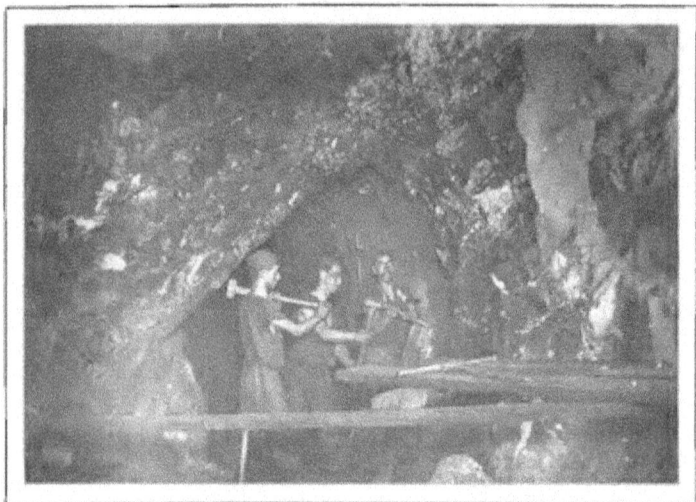

5.—THE 355 STOPES, COOK'S KITCHEN MINE.

6.—BORING AN UPPER, EAST POOL MINE.

8.—Underhand Stoping, East Pool Mine.

7.—Overhand Stoping, Cook's Kitchen Mine.

10.—THE 373 AT DOLCOATH MINE.

9.—THE 180 AT EAST POOL MINE.

Stoping is either "overhand" or "underhand." In the former case, the ground which has to be stoped is above the miners: in the latter, it is under them.

No. 7.—OVERHAND STOPING AT 335, COOK'S KITCHEN MINE.—More or less staging is necessary in overhand stoping, and the nearer the lode approaches the vertical, the more elaborate the staging becomes. Ladders are sometimes required to reach the staging easily, and are often used as a part of the staging itself. The water-box, with supply of spare borers, &c., is shown.

No. 8.—UNDERHAND STOPING AT 170, EAST POOL MINE.—The picture well illustrates a large underhand stope. One man is using the pick, and two "pares" are boring holes for blasting.

THE MINE AFTER EXPLOITATION.

Great caution is necessary, not only in deciding upon the general method of working the mine, but in carrying out numerous details which require careful consideration as work progresses from day to day. Veinstuff must be removed in such a way that the daily operations of tramming, &c. are not unduly interrupted. The safety of the employés has to be considered. Main roads have to be maintained. Ventilation must not be impeded. On many of the large lodes the excavations are on an extensive scale.

No. 9.—IN THE 180 AT EAST POOL MINE.—The lode here has been worked away for a considerable length and height. The walls are fairly secure and do not require much support. The tram-road is maintained in good order, and ladder communication with the levels below and above is available.

No. 10.—THE 375 NEAR NEW EAST SHAFT, DOLCOATH MINE.—In some portions of the deeper workings in Dolcoath, very treacherous ground has been met with, and the hanging-wall has been the cause of much trouble. At the spot shown in the photograph a big "run" occurred some time ago, a large quantity of stuff having fallen from above, down through the old workings, carrying tram-road and everything else with it. It was necessary to maintain tram-road communication here, and, as illustrated, massive pieces of wood were slung in chains from above, lowered to the required point, and the chains firmly secured. On these pieces a new tram-road was constructed which remains in constant use. The camera was placed some distance under the tram-road. The lode at this point has been taken away for a width varying from 20 to 30 feet.

No. 11.—THE 70 TRAM-ROAD AT EAST POOL MINE.—The lode here has been extensively wrought. The picture shows a suspicious part of the road propped by three pieces of Norway pine.

No. 12.—THE 17a RETURN, EAST POOL MINE.—A bridge has been constructed in order to take the wagons over a place where the lode has been stoped.

No. 13.—STOPING AT THE 70, EAST POOL MINE.—This picture shows another large stope in East Pool. The details are easily understood.

SUPPORTS.

Where the rock is soft, or the walls weak, supports have to be used. An absence of supports in No. 13 shows that the rock at the point illustrated is firm, and the roof strong.

No. 14.—DOLCOATH MINE, 412 LEVEL.—Supports of a massive character are shown here. The lode is of great width, is exceedingly rich, and the walls cannot always be relied upon. Hence great expense is incurred in timber. It is readily understood that skilled labour is required in dealing with such supports as those shown. The Dolcoath tributers are thoroughly capable men. Their workmanship in the deepest and most difficult parts of the mine does them credit. It is interesting to note that the winze which is sunk under the point where a bucket is shown in the plate yielded about one third black tin. "Every third kibble of stuff was clean tin," as one of the miners remarked. Near this spot the lode for its entire width is worth £5,000 per fathom, the "richest tin lode ever reported in the County of Cornwall."

[Since the remarks relating to plate No. 14 were written, the place shown in that plate has been the scene of a terrible disaster, in which seven men, including the foreman timberman at Dolcoath, lost their lives. The accident was rendered all the more sensational as one of the seven conversed with the rescuing party twenty hours after the accident and subsequently succumbed to his injuries altogether out of reach in the *débris*, and an eighth man was rescued unhurt after thirty-seven hours' entombment. The stull collapsed while it was being strengthened on September 20th, 1893, the large timbers being crushed and splintered out of shape. At the inquest, held at Camborne, on October 9th, when a verdict of "Accidental death" was returned and a vote of sympathy with the relatives of the deceased men and with the mine officials

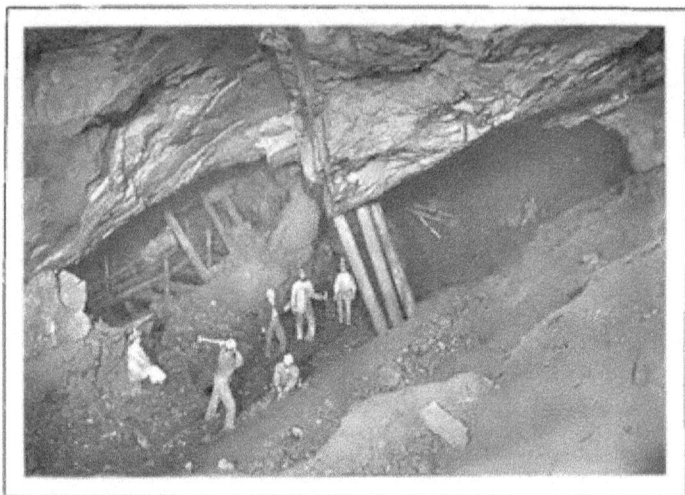

11.—THE 70 TRAM-ROAD, EAST POOL MINE.

12.—THE BRIDGE, EAST POOL MINE.

13.—STOPING AT THE 70. EAST POOL MINE.

14.—THE 412, DOLCOATH MINE.

was passed, the Manager, Capt. Josiah Thomas stated:—"The lode becomes larger as depth is attained, and in the deeper workings east of the engine shaft it is 20 or 30 feet wide with an underlie of 48° south, or a little over four feet in the fathom. The "country" on both sides is granite. In stoping away the lode we sometimes leave arches standing, and where arches are not left we put in large timbers across the workings at about right angles to the underlie of the lode. The timber used for this purpose is principally pitchpine 18 to 20 inches in diameter, propped when considered necessary by pitchpine or large pieces of Norway timber 12 to 16 inches in diameter." The stull shown in plate No. 14 consisted of 21 or 22 pieces of pitchpine, about 18 inches square, and about 33 or 34 feet in length. They were fixed two or three feet apart and at an angle of 45° to 48°. Naturally such an accident creates discussion upon the method of exploitation in vogue and also upon the principles upon which the timberwork is constructed. As the width of the main lode in Dolcoath has gradually increased in depth, special means of supporting the long pieces have been employed, and all local mining authorities are agreed that the collapsed stull was capable of bearing a much heavier strain than any which ordinarily could have come upon it. The cause of the collapse is not quite clear. Possibly an error in the judgment of the men, who were employed in strengthening a portion of the stull which was thought to require additional support, may have caused them to seriously weaken the foot of an old piece before the new piece was in its allotted position. Or a sudden and unexpected pressure from the hanging-wall—often an "unknown quantity"—may have asserted itself. A question which cropped up at the inquest, and which is receiving due consideration, is whether in a lode of such proportions it is desirable to maintain such wide levels and open spaces. Veins of great width are not of frequent occurrence in Cornwall, and, turning to those mining centres where the extraordinary width of vein forms a prominent feature, it is seen that the general practice is to avoid large chambers within the vein, and vast open spaces, as far as possible, is often being thought desirable to resort to various methods of obtaining waste material to fill such spaces. In the Santa Gertrudis Mine, Pachuca, Mexico, crosscuts are driven into the "country" to obtain the "filling." At the Cabezas del Pasto cupriferous iron pyrites mine in Southern Spain, quartzite is specially quarried at surface and sent down two special shafts to fill the portions of the deposit excavated. At some of the Stassfurt mines the impure rock salt is mined and sent back under those areas previously mined for salt of purer quality, where subsidence would cause much damage. The width and the inclination of the deposit, the nature of the foot- and hanging-wall, the uniformity of productiveness, and other considerations, determine the method of operations, and, naturally, opinions of mining engineers may seriously differ as to the best method to be applied to any particular vein or bed.]

No. 15.—BLUE HILLS MINE, STOPES ABOVE THE 66.—The lode here is about four or five feet wide and is exceedingly flat. Ladders are not generally required. The lode is so flat that the men easily walk on the foot-wall. The roof usually is pretty firm, and it is found that an occasional prop is all that is required to keep it in position. A "pare" of men is shown posting in a new prop.

No. 16.—ABOVE THE 306, COOK'S KITCHEN MINE.—In this instance the hanging-wall is very weak, and, while the method of supporting it is the same as that adopted at Blue Hills (see No. 15), the props, or posts, required for the purpose are more numerous. The lode underlies at an angle of about 45°. At and about the 306 the hanging wall has been very troublesome. It has occasioned two or three rather large "runs," and, unfortunately, some fatal accidents have been caused by falls of the hanging-wall, a fruitful source of serious accident in all mining operations.

DEEP MINING.

Dolcoath is the deepest mine in Cornwall, its neighbour Cook's Kitchen being the second deepest. Unfortunately neither mine possesses a downright shaft, a misfortune that becomes more painfully evident every year. From comparatively shallow depths the shafts have been sunk on the course of the lode in every instance.

15.—THE 66, BLUE HILLS MINE.

16.—ABOVE THE 406, COOK'S KITCHEN MINE.

17.—Engine Shaft at the 406, Cook's Kitchen Mine.

18.—The Bottom of Cook's Kitchen Engine Shaft.

20.—A MILL AT THE 412, DOLCOATH MINE.

19.—A ROCK-DRILL END, EAST POOL MINE.

No. 17.—The 406 Level, Engine Shaft, Cook's Kitchen Mine.—At the time the photograph was taken, the shaft was being sunk below the 406. Since then the 430 has been reached, and the latter level is now being driven east by rock-drill. The pumps, and the iron pipe conveying compressed air to the rock-drill at the bottom, show the rate of underlie. In the bow left corner of the plate a portion of the skip-road is to be seen. An air-winch is fixed to draw the stuff from the bottom of the shaft.

No. 18.—Bottom of Cook's Kitchen Shaft.—To obtain this view, the camera was fixed on the foot-wall at an angle of about 45°, the average underlie of the shaft. One has to imagine that he is looking down at this angle on the men in the bottom in order to appreciate the picture. The castings show the bottom of the bucket lift in the water at the bottom of the shaft. The flexible hose connects the air main shown in No. 17, to one of Messrs. Holmans Brothers' "Cornish" rock-drills, by means of which the shaft has been sunk. The drill, as is customary in Cornwall, is fixed on a stretcher bar, and is a 3½-inch machine. The "Cornish" drill has accomplished a large amount of useful work in the county.

No. 19.—East Pool Mine.—This plate shows a boring machine mounted on a stretcher bar for driving an end.

No. 20.—Dolcoath Mine, 412 Level.—A mill, or pass, into which the broken stuff is passed from stopes, or the level, above, and thence filled into tram wagons to be conveyed to the shaft.

HEAVES.

The difficulties of mining are, in some Cornish districts, increased by faults or heaves, the wrought vein being dislocated by another, and more recent, vein. There are instances of the lode being heaved fifty, and even more, fathoms by a "crosscourse," a vein which courses across the bearing of the lodes of the district, approximately at right angles. Crosscourse heaves are plan heaves, so called to distinguish them from section heaves, which are caused by veins running approximately parallel to the veins faulted, but having a greater or lower, or an opposite, underlie. Reference has already been made to the interesting group of heaves in the St. Agnes district. The writer has endeavoured, with the kind assistance of Capt. J. Richards, of Blue Hills, to obtain some plates in which the relative positions of the dislocated lode and the faulting vein are plainly marked, but the results are not quite satisfactory. Naturally, where the lode is only about five feet wide, the extent of the workings is limited. The space available for the camera is consequently small, so small that it was impossible to select good positions from which to photograph the heaves. Two of the best results obtained are given in numbers 21 and 22.

No. 21 was taken at Blue Hills, between the 30 and the 66, looking west. A large prop, which appears in the centre of the plate, came in the foreground, and could not be got rid of. This rather spoils the picture. The faulting vein, which consists almost entirely of white quartz, containing crystals of iron pyrites and a little copper ore, may be traced from behind the top of the prop in a slanting direction towards the low left corner. The men in the right half of the picture are boring a hole in the lode immediately underneath the foot-wall of the faulting vein. The latter throws the lode down south about eight or nine feet, and its position, south of the fault, may be judged from the appearance of the props which support the roof on the extreme left.

No. 22 is also from Blue Hills. It was taken in the back of the 66 looking east, and again shows the lode thrown down south, which here is on the right instead of on the left, the camera facing an opposite direction. The faulting vein is not so plainly marked, the quartz, of which it is mainly composed, being much darker in color. Its position may, however, be easily followed by the aid of the friendly light of the candle held close to its foot-wall. From the candle it runs upward to the centre of the plate. On the left, that is north of the fault, the prop, which is fixed at approximately right angles to the plane of the lode, shows the underlie. Two men are boring at, or very near, the point where the lode is cut off. On the south of the slide the lode is heaved down about 11 feet. The direction and extent of the heave may be judged from the relative positions of the men on both sides of the faulting vein.

No. 23 is a photograph of four stones from the St. Agnes district, and now in the writer's possession. That numbered 1 exhibits a series of small parallel veins of tinstone and quartz in slate. These small veins or branches, often no thicker than a knife blade, occur commonly in some portions of the district. At Polberro, many years since, a large section of ground of this character was worked in the open, an example of a tin stockwork. Some number 4 shows a heave of one vein by another in the stone, the whole being sufficiently plain without any explanation. The heaves throughout St. Agnes are, like that in the stone, caused by the descent of the hanging-wall. At West Kitty Mine an exploratory cross-cut at the 60 is, at the present time, exciting much interest at St. Agnes, as it is discovering the faulted upper portion of a lode from the deeper portions of which West Kitty has made a continuous run of dividends for the past fifteen years. This cross-cut is simply confirming the old

21.—HEAVE, LOOKING WEST, BLUE HILLS MINE.

22.—HEAVE, LOOKING EAST, BLUE HILLS MINE.

23—GROUP OF ST. AGNES ROCK SPECIMENS.

24—END OF GROUND AT THE OLD COOK'S KITCHEN MINE.

experience of the hanging-wall descent, and is making the prospects at West Kitty very pleasant, since every heave gives the mine more of the lode. The walls of the faulting vein are sometimes polished by the motion which produces the heave. Stones exhibiting this natural polish are called slickensides. No. 2 is one of these slickensides, the polished side being the lower. Very remarkable examples of breccia occur in the immediate vicinity of some of the veins. Occasionally the fragments are very large. In some number 3 the fragments are small, but the stone is a very pretty one of the class and recently came from the rock enclosing one of the Polberro lodes.

Undoubtedly the St. Agnes group of heaves has been caused by motion so slow as to be imperceptible. The lines of fault are approximately east and west. They divide the disturbed belt into an innumerable number of sections, which are north and south to one another. It is uniformly seen that the general effect has been to depress each south section relatively to its adjacent section to the north, or, in other words, to elevate each north section relatively to its adjacent section to the south. The regularity which this would seem to produce is occasionally apparently upset by very flat slides of a more recent date than, and having an underlie opposite to, the principal faulting veins. But, while such occurrences may interfere with the preconceived notions of those who expect to see faulted veins follow the lines accorded to them in ideal or prospective cross sections, they in no way form an exception to the general rule which governs the group of heaves at St. Agnes. Whatever the direction of the underlie may be, the hanging-wall invariably descends relatively to the foot-wall. Consequently it is not difficult to determine the *direction* of a heave at St. Agnes, except in rare cases, for example, where the faulting vein so nearly approaches the perpendicular that one cannot distinguish between the hanging-and-foot-walls. The solution of the West Kitty case (*see page 30*) is easy. It is absolutely safe to predict that the dislocated upper portion of the lode will be discovered in the 60 cross-cut. The *extent* of the heave is quite another matter. This varies from a few inches up to 15 or 20 fathoms, or more in exceptional cases.

The remaining photographs require very little explanation.

No. 24.—COOK'S KITCHEN MINE. THE 355 EAST.—In this "end of ground" the bunded structure of the lode is very plainly illustrated, and for this reason the plate has been selected for publication.

In No. 35, the miners are enjoying the usual "croust* time,' having performed the first part of the day's labour. Some of the holes bored are often blasted before "croust," so that the smoke may clear away while the welcome and well-earned "crib" and pipe are being enjoyed.

No. 26, the interior of the museum at the Camborne Mining School, appropriately brings the series to a close.

The centre cases in the museum contain what is known as the "Taylor" collection of minerals, which was presented to the school in 1892 by Mr. J. C. Williams, M.P., then President of The Mining Association and Institute of Cornwall. This collection is a very complete one, consisting of over 6,000 specimens, and is particularly rich in old and rare Cornish minerals. Characteristic collections from such important and well-known mining districts as Kimberley, Rio Tinto, Real del Monte, Mysore, Ookiep, &c., form an interesting feature in the museum. The school laboratory is on the next floor, immediately above the museum, and is of the same liberal dimensions.

---

* CROUST, Cornish Celtic for an afternoon meal.

25.—"CROUST TIME," EAST POOL MINE.

26.—MUSEUM, CAMBORNE MINING SCHOOL.

www.ingramcontent.com/pod-product-compliance
Lightning Source LLC
Chambersburg PA
CBHW021543270326
41930CB00008B/1340